31 DAYS OF JUST JESUS

Copyright © 2019 by Stephanie M. White

ISBN-13: 978-0-9896973-3-0

This book was printed in the United States of America.

HTTPS://WHITESTEPHANIE83.WIXSITE.COM/ HEAVENONEARTHFORYOU

What would happen if we decided to focus our thoughts solely on Jesus? No matter where our thoughts wandered, we chose to redirect them back to Christ? Our lives would be transformed; that is what would happen.

> Isaiah 26:3 (KJV) Thou wilt keep him in perfect peace, whose mind is stayed on Thee: because he trusteth in Thee.

What does it mean to have a mind that is "stayed" on Christ? This word was translated from a Hebrew word that paints a vivid picture for us through its various definitions. The descriptive definitions include: to prop, to lean upon, to lay, to rest self and set self, to take hold of, to establish, to stand fast, to stay (self), to sustain. A mind that is "stayed" on Christ is established and sustained by Christ. The person who focuses their thoughts on Christ leans upon the Word and is supported by the Word (and don't forget, the Word is Christ - John 1:1). The person who focuses their thoughts on Christ finds personal rest in Him. They are established and can stand fast no matter the circumstances because they are not focused on self, but on Christ.

Focusing on Christ rather than self is a learning process; a mind that is in step with the Spirit doesn't just happen overnight. Every Spiritual learning process requires time in the Word of God. As we fill ourselves with the Seed of the Word, the fruit of Christ-centeredness will be produced. We are self-centered because we ignore the Word or we look at the Word incorrectly. Reading the Word as a rule book will cause us to become self-absorbed. We will continually focus on self if we view the Word as something to be conquered or as rules we cannot live up to. When we look at the Word and try to change ourselves to fit into the mold of how we view the Word, we will fail. Either we will see our inadequacies and live in self-loathing and guilt or we will erroneously believe that we are well-performing achievers and live in arrogance and judgment of others - either way, we are focused on self. Reading the Word as the Spiritual Seed that it truly is will cause us to live focused on Christ. We will understand that He is the Source of all things Spiritual and apart from Him we can do nothing of Spiritual value. When we live this way, Jesus truly increases in our lives and our carnal nature decreases.

As we look into the process of renewing our minds and making Christ our focus, we must gauge where we are now. To what degree is my mind "stayed" on Christ? Am I leaning heavily on Him or am I propping myself up with (what I view as) good works, worldly philosophies, or excuses? Am I abiding in His Word, thus being sustained by Him, or am I trying to live the Christian life without Christ (the Word)? Am I at rest in His presence or am I anxious and worried about many things? Am I trying to change myself or am I taking hold of the Seed of the Word and relying on Him to produce Spiritual fruit in my life?

The condition of your mind determines the condition of your life. As a man thinks, so he becomes (Proverbs 23:7 KJV). Our thought life is imperative. If I believe I must impress God with my behavior, then I will be focused on self; on the other hand, if I believe that Christ alone can produce Spiritual fruit in my life, I will then choose to focus on Him. Each way of thinking will produce fruit, but only one way of thinking will produce *Spiritual* fruit. We need more of Him and less of self if we want to see a Spiritual transformation in our lives.

The mind that is focused on Christ is kept peaceful. Peace of mind is something everyone longs for, but the majority find elusive. Isaiah describes peace as perfect peace in our English translation; in the Hebrew it is simply peace, peace. A double dose of peace. Who wouldn't want seconds when it comes to peace? The Hebrew word that was translated as "peace" is *shalom*. It is one of the more recognizable Hebrew words and it is a beautiful description of what Christ has prepared for us. This word, and its various facets, describes everything we could possibly want and everything that is already ours in Christ: safety, well-being, happiness, friendliness, welfare, good health, prosperity, tranquility, favor, rest, wholeness. These descriptors are amazing in themselves, but keep in mind to double them! Who wouldn't want to live with double *shalom*? No one in their right mind...awe, there is the rub. The mind is the heart of the matter. Our minds keep us from this life of *shalom* squared but that is actually good news because we can do something about that. We can change our minds! We have that powerful privilege. *You* are in control of what you choose to focus your thoughts on.

> 2 Corinthians 10:5 (NIV) We demolish arguments and every pretension that sets itself up against the knowledge of God, and we take captive every thought to make it obedient to Christ.

This one verse can change your life if you understand it. God is telling you, child of God, that you have the power to make your thoughts obey Christ. That means you have the power to demolish anything that claims to be more powerful in your life than God. Wow! That is amazing! Anything that disagrees with God's promises for your life has no power unless you give it power - your God-given power.

God tells us in the previous verse that this is part of waging war. "Waging war" is our spoiler alert - this will not be a walk in the park. Renewing our minds and having a mind that is "stayed" on Christ will take us to new places, but it will also take us through some rough places along the way. In the same way the children of Israel had to forge across the desert before entering the promised land, our journey to a mind that is "stayed" on Christ will be full of its challenges, battles, and dry patches. But be of good cheer.

God has told us that we do not wage war like the world does. We wage war with a Weapon that cannot be destroyed or defeated - the Living Word of God, Jesus Christ Himself. We have been given this Weapon but it is up to us to wield it. What you do with the Word of God determines how much of Christ's victory you will experience this side of eternity. God wants you to experience heaven on earth now - why wait? You can live a life of double *shalom* by exercising your mind Spiritually. As you consistently take in the Word of God, something happens. Your mental muscles are strengthened. You become stronger Spiritually and your flesh becomes weaker. The weaker the flesh becomes, the less it torments you. That sounds wonderful, doesn't it? Why wait any longer to renew your mind?

This journey cannot be rushed. Faith is a process and it takes time - time spent in the Word reading, meditating, speaking, and praying. This journey cannot be rushed but it can be prolonged. The more you abide in the Word, the farther along the Spiritual path you will be; however, if you choose to ignore the Spiritual battle we all face and refuse to wage war with your weapon of the Word, you will remain in your depraved state of mind.

For the next 31 days we are going to learn more about the person who focuses their thoughts on Christ and we are going to learn how to be that person, more importantly.

For a free set of companion workbook sheets, visit:

**https://whitestephanie83.wixsite.com/
heavenonearthforyou**

GOD LOVES ME

Jesus Christ came into the world because He loves us. He created us because He loves us. He paid the price for our sin because He loves us. A mind that is stayed on Christ is a mind that is focused on His purpose - His love for us.

We cannot renew our minds without starting with salvation. We must know how we are saved and why. We are saved because we accept what Christ did for us - and He did it because He loves us. We can only receive forgiveness of sins by agreeing that we are sinners and acknowledging Jesus' loving payment for our sins and receiving it. He loves us that much! He was buried and rose again on the third day declaring that His payment was

John 3:16-17 (KJV)
For God so loved the world, that He gave His only begotten Son, that whosoever believeth in Him should not perish, but have everlasting life.
For God sent not His Son into the world to condemn the world, but that the world through Him might be saved.

accepted by the Father as payment in full. His resurrection declared loud and clear that we could now walk in newness of life, guilt-free Spiritual life, here on earth and for eternity in heaven.

Too many times we believe salvation is based on us. We come up with all of our own theories on how to earn what only Christ freely gives. We decide we must be good enough to get to heaven. We must do some kind of service to receive forgiveness and deserve blessings. And so on. Religion is man's idea of God's plan - not God's. That is why Jesus declared His contempt for religion. Jesus does not want us to be religious; He wants us to have an intimate relationship with Him - and the two are polar opposites. For example, religion tells us that *we* must do some "good" work to deserve something from God; Jesus tells us that we must receive from Him and then we will be equipped to produce good works or, more accurately put, *Spiritual* fruit. Religion tells us that God is angry and He is waiting to punish us for our sins so we better try real hard to appease Him; Jesus tells us that God is pleased with us (because of Jesus) and we can walk at liberty and ease knowing that He took our punishment (Isaiah 53:5).

His love for us is based on Christ - not us. More of Him, less of me.

GOD REALLY LOVES ME

God loves me and I am worthy of His love. This may be hard to swallow at times but it is true nonetheless. We erroneously assume this cannot be true when we are not at our best, but there we go again focusing on self rather than Christ. We are worthy of His love because *Christ* made us worthy. We have the right to experience the love of God at *all* times because of Christ. We cannot focus on self and realize His love for us at the same time.

Do not fall for the lie that says you must deserve His love because no one could ever do that. There is nothing you can do to earn God's love - it is a free gift. Even our love for Him is a free gift: We

Ephesians 3:17-19 (NIV)

...that Christ may dwell in your hearts through faith...I pray that you, being rooted and established in love, may have power...to grasp how wide and long and high and deep is the love of Christ, and to know this love that surpasses knowledge - that you may be filled to the measure of all the fullness of God.

love Him because He first loved us (1 John 4:19).

What makes us believe we could be worthy of His love at all? Even when we are at our best, the Word tells us that our righteousness is of no value (Romans 3:10).

God wants us to realize His love for us. He wants us to be rooted in His love. This means our foundation must be His love for us. As we live our daily lives as Christians we must remind ourselves of His love. I believe it is a great idea to make a list of verses that express God's love for you so that you can read them every single day. We let our loved ones tell us that they love us regularly, why not let God do the same?

We are told that knowing God's love makes us full. So many people are living life on empty and because of their sad state; they are looking to others to fill them up. This puts unnecessary pressure on those around you. No one can ever fill you like Christ can. We will never feel complete without His love.

If our minds are going to remain stayed on Christ, we must learn how to avoid focusing on self in every area. The enemy wants us to be self-absorbed because it is the loneliest, most depressing, joyless life there is. More of Him, less of me - that is the life of the person whose mind is stayed on Him and that is an abundant life!

I AM RIGHTEOUS

2 Corinthians 5:21 (NIV)

God made Him who had no sin to be sin for us, so that in Him we might become the righteousness of God.

I am righteous. This single statement makes our legalistic, carnal nature cringe. This single statement sparks heated debate in the Christian community and especially the religious community. How dare we claim to be righteous? We dare, because He first proclaimed it loudly and clearly in His Word. We are righteous - but we are righteous only because of what HE did for us.

Righteousness is not something we can achieve on our own. The Bible tells us that if we break one part of the law, we are guilty of breaking it all (James 2:10). God is showing us that we can never achieve righteousness on our own. We have a sinful nature and our sinful nature sins. That should be easy to understand but it's not always the case. Many times we struggle with why we sin. We don't understand how we can do some of the things we do. We feel stressed and guilty because we sin. These feelings are not our friends. These feelings push us away from God. These feelings keep the focus on self and not on Christ.

We sin. Why? We sin because we are ignoring the Word of God in our lives. We sin because we are focused on self rather than Christ. That is it - there is not some complicated reason behind it. It is that simple and there is a simple solution. The Bible tells us to hide the Word of God in our heart so that we won't sin (Psalm 119:11). The Word keeps us from sin. If we are walking in the Spirit, we cannot fulfill the lusts of our flesh (Galatians 5:16).

More of Him, less of me. I must realize that I cannot make myself righteous; I am already righteous because of what Christ did for me. A mind that is stayed on Christ is focused on what *He* has done. As my mind focuses on Christ, I will begin to see myself as He does. I will realize who I truly am because my heavenly Father loves me so much. I am the righteousness of God in Christ because of His great love. He took my place so I could receive His righteousness. Why would we want to focus on anything else?

I AM FORGIVEN

I am forgiven. A mind that is stayed on Him is a mind that is stayed on forgiveness, as well. My forgiveness was established by Christ when He paid the price for my sins. I can lean on Him and rest in what He has done for me. I can rest in what He says about me. He has removed my transgressions from me. He did that so I no longer need to focus on myself or my sin.

More of Him, less of me. More of what He did for me by removing my sins as far as the east is from the west. If I choose to focus on what He has done to remove my sins, then I won't have time to focus on committing sin.

A mind that is stayed on

Psalm 103:12 (NIV) As far as the east is from the west, so far has He removed our transgressions from us.

Isaiah 43:25 (NIV) ...I am He who blots out your transgressions ...and remembers your sin no more.

Christ is a mind that is at peace. When I focus on my sin, I am lacking peace. Sin never brings anything positive into your life. The Bible tells us the way of the transgressor is hard (Proverbs 13:15). Sin never profits us. It is a destructive force that Christ set us free from. It is interesting to look at the Hebrew word that was translated as transgressor in our English Bible. The Hebrew word is defined as: to cover; to deal deceitfully, to act covertly; to pillage. As we look at this definition and ponder its meaning, we see that the transgressor is undercover; they are dealing deceitfully with themselves by covering up who they really are. The transgressor is focused on self and not on who they are in Christ. When we ignore our Spiritual identity, life is hard. We are robbing ourselves of every good thing Jesus has already attained for us.

We are in a Spiritual war. The enemy wants you to live defeated. He wants you to feel sorry for yourself and immerse yourself in guilt. If he can get you to do that, then he has won; however, God's Word tells us we are more than conquerors. We do not have to fall for the enemy's lies when we know the truth!

More of Him, less of me. I need to focus my thoughts on what He says about me. The Word boldly declares that I'm forgiven. Who am I to live like I am not?

I AM COMPLETELY FORGIVEN

I am completely forgiven for everything. I was taught that I was only forgiven for the things I did before I was saved; after I received Christ, however, I would have to answer for my sin. This way of thinking negates the cleansing power of the blood and it keeps us from truly embracing the love of God.

If we walk in the light, we will understand that the blood of Jesus has *completely* purified us. Walking in the light is walking in the Word. It is walking in the truth of the Word. If the Word tells us that our sins are to be remembered no more, then that is what we need to focus on. Many times we look at other verses that

> *1 John 1:7 (NIV)*
>
> *But if we walk in the light, as He is in the light, we have fellowship with one another, and the blood of Jesus, His Son, purifies us from all sin.*

are being addressed to people who have not accepted Christ and we apply them to ourselves - this will keep us in a state of confusion. If I read a letter written by my neighbor to his wife, I would never be able to completely understand it; however, if I was reading a letter my husband wrote to me, I would understand it. I would know what he meant because I know him. When we know God and His love for us, we will know when a verse is addressed to us and when a verse is not addressed to us. As a child of God, we will be able to distinguish between what is addressed to the unsaved and what is addressed to the saved. Do not read a verse that says your sins have kept you from God and apply that to yourself. This does not apply to the child of God whose sins have been removed by Jesus Christ. Do not belittle what Christ did by identifying with sin.

Walk in the light. More of Him, less of me. As we continue to renew our minds and focus them on Christ, we will see that He is the source of every good thing. Forgiveness is a good thing. Forgiveness sets us free; it brings joy; it enables us to forgive others. Keep your mind set on what Christ has done for you rather than what you have done or what someone else has done. A double dose of peace can be yours! Choose your thoughts wisely.

NO FEAR OF PUNISHMENT

I do not have to fear punishment. This does not mean that God is soft on sin or He doesn't care. The punishment for my sin was taken by Jesus Christ. Jesus Christ bled and died for our sins - He did not die a "soft" death. If we look at what Christ went through, then we will no longer believe that God is soft on sin; rather, we will recognize the wages of sin and live thankful that Christ paid the price for us. As we keep our focus on Christ, we will understand that our righteousness is a loving gift.

Punishment makes us fearful. It keeps us from intimacy with God. No one draws near to someone they are afraid of.

Romans 3:23-25 (NLT)

...we all fall short of God's glorious standard. Yet God, with undeserved kindness, declares that we are righteous. He did this through Christ Jesus when He freed us from the penalty for our sins. For God presented Jesus as the sacrifice for sin. People are made right with God when they believe that Jesus sacrificed His life, shedding His blood...

When we do not understand that Christ paid the price for our sin in full, we will be left feeling like we still deserve some sort of punishment. This feeling will not draw us to God. This feeling is the result of self-absorption. This feeling is the result of choosing to ignore what Christ did for us and instead focusing on what we have done.

When we live life fearful of God's vengeance, we are living life disregarding Christ's sacrifice. In essence, we are declaring that what Christ did was not enough and that there is still a balance due by us. These thoughts are in direct contrast to the Word of God. It is time to wage war on these thoughts and make them obey the Word.

More of Him and less of me. Less focus on what I have done wrong and more focus on what He has done right. As we choose to fix our thoughts on Christ and lean on Him, we will begin to experience Spiritual fruit in every area. The person who realizes what Christ did for them is the person who is walking in the Spirit. Our spirit cannot sin; it is impossible. His loving sacrifice forgives our sins and keeps us away from sin. He is so good to us!

The next time you are tempted to fear punishment, take the time to remind yourself of Christ's payment. Remind yourself that Christ took the punishment you deserved because of His unfailing love for you.

I RELY ON GOD'S LOVE

I can solely rely on God's love for me. I do not have to make an attempt to rely on myself.

I will fail time and time again, but God's love is unfailing. As we saw on day 6, the fear of punishment keeps us from God, but His perfect love will keep us from fearing punishment. His perfect love will keep us in awe of God and keep us focused on Him rather than self.

Know the love of God. How can we know His love? We can know His love by becoming familiar with it in His Word. I hope you have made a list of verses that declare God's love for you and I hope you are taking them in daily. The more you read about His love, the more you will know His love. An intimate

> *1 John 4:16-19 (NIV)*
>
> *And so we know and rely on the love God has for us...There is no fear in love. But perfect love drives out fear because fear has to do with punishment.*

knowledge of His love takes time and it requires relational living. God wants to be in a loving relationship with you - are you in agreement with His plan?

Rely on the love of God. Rely - to rely on God's love means to have faith in God's love. Faith is the end result of our intake of the Word (Romans 10:17). If we want to rely on God's love for us, then we need to fill ourselves with God's love for us. As we take in His Word on His love for us, we begin to know His love and this knowledge will lead to reliance. If you will do that one simple thing, so many other things in your life will fall into place. Knowing His love will lead us to depend on His love and we will lean on Him instead of trying to make ourselves stand.

The love of God drives out fear. We cannot live in fear and live in love simultaneously. Fear is debilitating and it will keep us from the good things of God. Fearing punishment will definitely keep us in doubt regarding the blessings of God. We must realize what the fear of punishment does to us and we must wage war on this mindset of the flesh.

Keep your mind stayed on Him. More of Him, less of you. Lean on what He's done for you. Prop yourself up under His loving arms and refuse to let fear control you.

Day 8

I IGNORE THE ENEMY

I have the power to ignore the threats of the enemy. Instead of complaining and feeling beat up because the enemy is attacking, I can choose to ignore the threats. I can choose to hear nothing. I have the power to choose. I do not have to entertain the threats. Anything that is contrary to the Word of God is a threat and I have *the* Weapon that will neutralize every threat.

Why do we give the enemy our attention? Why do we give our attention to things that disagree with the Word? We do so because we choose to. Many people will not like that answer or even agree with it, but that does not mean it is not true. I am in control of what I choose to dwell on. If the enemy

Psalms 38:13-15 (NLT)

But I am deaf to all their threats, I am silent before them as one who cannot speak. I choose to hear nothing & I make no reply. For I am waiting on You, Lord. You must answer me, O Lord my God.

threatens me that does not mean I have to meditate on that threat. I have the power to ignore it. My power comes from the Word of God. The Word is my weapon in defeating the lies of the enemy.

More of Him (the Word), less of me. I must remember that some days *I* am my own worst enemy. Some days *I* am the one feeding myself the lies. I am my own worst enemy when I focus more on my circumstances than I do the Word.

The power to ignore the lies of the enemy comes from our decision to *wait* on the Lord. When we look at this word we see it was translated from a Hebrew word that means to be patient, to stay, to tarry. It is describing the person whose mind is stayed on Christ - the person who is focused on the Word no matter the circumstances. More of Him, less of me, and then I can ignore the lies of the enemy. Just Jesus - no more of the lies!

Are you deaf to the things that contradict the Word or do you give them your attention? We can be deaf to the things of the flesh if want to be - we have the power to choose the Word of God in our daily lives. We have the power, through Christ, to defeat the enemy and see victory.

CHRIST IS MY ADVOCATE

1 John 2:1 (NIV)

My dear children, I write this to you so that you will not sin. But if anybody does sin, we have an advocate with the Father - Jesus Christ, the Righteous One.

My advocate is Jesus Christ. What does this mean exactly? The Greek word for advocate means intercessor, consoler, comforter, supporter, promoter. An advocate is summoned, called to one's side, especially called to one's aid. An advocate is one who pleads another's cause; an intercessor; helper, an aide, assistant. What a description of who Christ is.

Jesus is for us - not against us - when we sin. He is there to help us and remind us that we have been forgiven. He is our atoning sacrifice. He has made up for every sin we will ever commit. We must be mindful of that! How many times do we feel the exact opposite? We feel as if God is nowhere to be found when we sin; we feel like there is a barrier between us. We feel this way because we are not familiar with the truth. We are not familiar with the fact that Jesus is our advocate.

Jesus is there for us when we sin. He is there to comfort us and call us to His side. He wants to help us get back to where we belong - in the Spirit. We sin because we are in the flesh. There are two parts to every one of us as Christians and we must realize the need to walk in the Spirit as opposed to the flesh. You are a child of God - a dearly loved child of God - and you do not have to live in the flesh. You have everything you need to live in the Spirit. You have the Word of God. Refuse to believe the lie that says Christ is not there for you when you sin. Wage war against this carnal mindset.

More of Him, less of me. More about His role as my advocate, less of me trying to take care of myself and fix myself. My mind is stayed on Him when I focus on who He is and who He is to me. I can ignore the lies of the flesh when I see the truth - Jesus is for me; He's not against me! Jesus is waiting for me to reach out and receive His unconditional love and support. He is waiting for me to receive from Him and walk in newness of life with Him. Just Jesus, no more guilt or condemnation!

I AM SPIRITUALLY FRUITFUL IN CHRIST

I am a fruit-bearer! In our quest to keep our minds stayed on Christ, we are learning to speak the truth instead of lies. Declare your ability to produce fruit even if you feel fruitless. You can declare your ability because Christ has. More of Him, less of you - more of what He says about you rather than how you perceive things. Keep your thoughts focused on what He says about you.

We will bear Spiritual fruit if we abide in Christ. He is our Source for all things Spiritual. Apart from Christ we can do nothing of Spiritual value. Too many times we get things twisted. We start to believe that we produce Spiritual fruit *for*

> *John 15:5 (NIV)*
>
> *I am the vine; you are the branches. If you remain in Me and I in you, you will bear much fruit; apart from Me you can do nothing.*

Christ instead of *through* Christ. If you begin to feel proud of yourself for the things "you" do, then you need a refresher course of John 15.

We are fruit-bearing Christians only because of our relationship with Christ. As we unite with Him, we begin to see ourselves as one with Him. We identify with who we are Spiritually instead of who we are on our own. This identity includes the ability to produce Spiritual fruit. If we choose to abide in Him, choose to make our dwelling place His Word, then Spiritual fruit will be produced naturally. Just like a branch will die if it is cut off from the vine, we, too, will live a dead life apart from Christ.

If your desire is to have a mind that is stayed on Christ, then this verse will be one of your favorites. It reminds us that we are of no Spiritual value apart from Him. It reminds us of our desperate need for Him. It reminds us that He is the Source of Spiritual life. This verse exemplifies the definition of "stayed" - we are fruitful when we are sustained and established by Christ, when we lean on Him and rest in Him rather than self. This verse reminds us to stand fast in the Word and to keep our minds stayed on Christ. It encourages us to look to Him rather than self. More of Him, less of me. This is the formula for life in the Spirit.

NO COMPARISON

I do not compare myself to others. When we have a mind that is stayed on Christ we will never feel the need to compare ourselves among ourselves. We will understand that we are unique and we are special.

Christ has made me special. Life can have a way of making us doubt that. As we live our daily lives, we encounter numerous opportunities to make comparisons. We are bombarded with social media images that portray false perfection. We are surrounded with magazines, billboards, movies, and the like, that airbrush and perfect flawed people. We even encounter people in our lives that seem to be ideal and have it all together. We must remember that appearances

2 Corinthians 10:12 (NIV)

We do not dare to classify or compare ourselves with some who commend themselves. When they measure themselves by themselves and compare themselves with themselves, they are not wise.

are many times deceiving.   I am sure you can think of plenty of times when things were not how you made them appear to everyone else.

We cannot live by appearances. Life is real. Life is difficult and it can be messy. We age, we fail, we struggle, and we suffer loss. These things happen, but they do not define us. We must choose to see ourselves based on what Christ says about us. A mind that is focused on Christ is not focused on self. A mind that is focused on Christ does not feel the need to play the comparison game.

We can live free of defeating comparisons by ignoring the temptation.   How do we ignore the temptation? We replace it. When we feel the temptation to compare ourselves among ourselves, we can choose to focus on what Christ says about our identity. We can choose to redirect our thoughts. Instead of thinking about the things we assume we lack, we can think about every good thing we have in Christ. We can choose to go to the Word, our infallible weapon. We can fight the temptation to compare and we can win through Christ!

More of Him, less of me. More of Him, less of others. More about who He is will teach me who I really am. When I see myself in Christ I will see I am complete and I cannot be compared with anyone else.

I AM FEARLESS IN CHRIST

I do not live fearful. Fear has no power over the person whose mind is stayed on Christ. Fear cannot control you when Christ is in control.

Fear will poke its ugly head into your life repeatedly, but you have what it takes to make fear take off running. You have the Word and the Word will demolish fear. Jehoshaphat was a human being just like you, just like me. He struggled with fear but he also understood how to defeat it. When fear came knocking, he went straight to the Lord. He was determined to defeat fear and he knew the only way to do so was through Christ.

2 Chronicles 20:3 (Amplified)

Then Jehoshaphat feared and set himself [determinedly, as his vital need] to seek the Lord.

Fear is the result of not being mindful of Jesus. We fear death because we forget that Christ conquered death and He is Life. We fear lack because we forget that God has promised to be our provider. We fear danger because we forget about the safety and security promised in the Word. We fear loss because we forget that Christ is our sufficiency. The list can go on and on, but we can begin to put a stop to fear one step at a time.

When you are tempted to fear, take the time to stop and think about *why* you are tempted to fear. The temptation has made its way into your life because of your thoughts and your circumstances. We may not be able to control our circumstances, but we sure can control our thoughts. We *can* make our thoughts obey the Word. We *can* choose to replace the thoughts of fear with the promises of God. This process is not for the lazy at heart. This process is just that - a process! And processes require time. We are already using our time to think about our problem, so let's choose to make better use of our time. Take the time you spend thinking about your problem and make a trade with that time. Choose to spend that time focusing on God's promises concerning your problem.

Fear can only control you as long as you let it. More of Him, less of me. No fear, just Jesus!

I AM GUILT-FREE IN CHRIST

I can live guilt-free. God has promised to set us free from guilt. When we focus solely on Jesus, guilt will have no room in our lives. Guilt is the result of focusing on self rather than Christ. Guilt interrupts our peace and joy because we give it our permission to do so. We do this by choosing to focus on our sin. We remind ourselves of all we have done wrong. We focus on our mistakes and how we have disappointed others rather than focusing on Christ's forgiveness.

We must truly understand the part that we play in our lives. When we believe that life just happens and we are helpless to change things, depression will set in. We cannot live joy-filled lives

Psalm 32:5 (NIV)

Then I acknowledged my sin to You and did not cover up my iniquity. I said, "I will confess my transgressions to the Lord." And You forgave the guilt of my sin.

when we are full of guilt, fear, insecurity, and the like. We must understand that these carnal feelings hang around because we let them. Instead of fighting them with the truth of the Word, we choose to dwell on them. We give them our precious time and then we wonder why we feel so miserable. Wonder no more - instead, begin to fight back!

Guilt has no rightful place in your life because of Jesus Christ. He paid the price for your sin and the result of your sin. Guilt, shame, and blame have been paid for by the blood of Jesus. Those feelings have no right to take up your time; they have no right to occupy space in your mind. Look up verses that declare you are forgiven and meditate on them. Think about them, speak them out loud, memorize them, and pray them. Use the weapon of the Word to defeat guilt in your life.

Guilt will defeat you if you do not defeat it. Guilt is a burden we were never designed to carry; it is overwhelming. Give this burden to Jesus. Refuse to carry it any longer and begin to feel the freedom that only He can give. Just Jesus - not your past, not your mistakes, not your guilt - just Jesus. Focus on Him and let guilt-ridden thoughts find a new home. More of Him, less of me. Less of my sin and shame and more of His glory and grace.

I AM NOT AFRAID OF THE DARK

John 1:4-5 (NIV)

In Him was life and that life was the light of all mankind. The light shines in the darkness and darkness cannot overcome it.

I am never in the dark when I am in His presence.

Why is darkness scary? Darkness keeps us guessing. We are not sure of what is right in front of us. Darkness encourages us to go by what we feel. When the lights suddenly go out in a room, our first instinct is to feel around. We lack vision so we trust our other senses. Darkness tempts us to trust our feelings. The problem with that is this: our feelings are fickle. One minute we feel one way and the next minute, we feel the opposite. We can be excited about an event one day and dread it the next day. Feelings cannot be trusted.

When we cannot see we tend to panic. Panic leads us to

make poor decisions. Panic is a feeling of helplessness and hopelessness. Panic comes in when we forget who our God is. He is the Light. In the same way we can shine a flashlight in a dark room, we can shine the Light of the Word in our dark circumstances.

Darkness represents evil. It's an absence of light and Christ is the Light. Darkness cannot overcome light. Light will always dispel darkness. Jesus Christ will always drive out evil. Too many times we try to drive out the darkness on our own. We come up with a plan and dive deeper into the darkness when it doesn't work. Trusting in our attempts is just like trusting in a flashlight without batteries. Christ is our power source. Without God's power, we'll never overcome the darkness of this life.

Just Jesus. Not my ideas, not my plans. Just Jesus. I need to keep my thoughts focused on Him and His promises for me. When darkness is approaching, I need to shine the Light of the Word immediately. Darkness cannot overcome my God - no matter what brand of darkness it may be.

More of Him, less of me. More of His light in this dark world. As I shine the Light of His Word, darkness has to flee. Darkness has no authority over His great Light.

I AM NOT AFRAID OF WHAT COULD BE

I do not live in fear of what might be. Our days are precious; we do not have time to worry about the possibility of something bad happening. There will always be threats but we can choose to listen to them and give them our attention, or we can fight them with the promises of God.

As we learned yesterday, light overcomes darkness; darkness cannot overcome light. Things may happen, but light will still overcome darkness. It would be foolish to say that bad things will never happen; suffering is real. Jesus told us that in this world we would have trials and tribulations, but He didn't stop there. He said that we could be of good cheer even

Jeremiah 51:46 (NIV)

Do not lose heart or be afraid when rumors are heard in the land; one rumor comes this year, another the next...

though we will experience hardships in this world because He has overcome this world (John 16:33). No matter what happens; He is greater. This life is temporary and so are the trials of this life. In contrast, His victory is eternal and we can begin to experience it now. We can set our minds on the things above and not on the things of this earth.

Rumors, threats, feelings, fears - all of these can be paralyzing and destructive. When we choose to ignore the promises of God, fears will take over and lead us down a dark path. When we think that something negative is going to happen, we are placing ourselves in enemy territory. We must realize that the fear of what could happen is a tool of the enemy and it will only be affective when we ignore the promises of God.

One of God's precious gifts to us is the ability to not lose heart and to be of good cheer. We can choose more of Him and less of the rumors, threats, and so on. We can set our minds on the Word of God. We can redirect our thoughts when they wander and make us fearful. We have that power thanks to Jesus Christ - what are we doing with it?

More of Him, less of me. Less of my doubts and fears and more of His promises. I do not need to fear tomorrow because my God is already there.

I AM NOT AFRAID OF TOMORROW

I am not afraid of what tomorrow holds. God tells me that I can laugh at the days to come; I do not have to fear them. Tomorrow is not promised to any of us, but if it does arrive, it will be nothing that we need to be afraid of. Our God is already there. He knows what tomorrow holds and He knows the plans He has for us. We can look to Him and focus on His promises regarding our lives and we can be confident and assured. We do not have to live in fear of what may come.

Fear is a theme we have discussed more than once because fear is a popular tool of the enemy. Fear has various forms. Fear of death, fear of the future, fear of sickness, fear of loss, fear

Proverbs 31:25 (NIV)

She is clothed with strength and dignity; she can laugh at the days to come.

of change, and so on. Fear is a billion dollar industry. Just look at the insurance industry. Its claim to take care of us IF something terrible were to happen makes us rush and sign up. Our fears make us desperate for what they are offering. We have "insurance" for everything but there is nothing that can *assure* us except for Jesus Christ!

Jesus Christ told us to look at the future and laugh. He told us to be of good cheer and not to worry about tomorrow. He boldly tells us these things because He has promised to be there for us no matter what. We live in a sinful world. Man chose to ignore God; consequently, sin prevails. Man's proclivity for sin keeps this world full of pain and hurt, but God is not shocked and He is not unsure about what to do next. God's plan for man is the same in good times as it is in bad times - keep your focus on the Word of God. This means that we are just as desperate for God on our best day as we are on our worst. We can laugh at tomorrow when our faith is in Him. When He is greater in our lives than fear, we will laugh.

Loss may come, but He is our restoration. Sickness may come, but He's our healer. Death may come, but it's only temporary thanks to Jesus. For each negative that this sinful world provides, Christ gives us an even greater promise. We need more of Him and less of our fear.

Day 17

MY LIFE GETS BETTER EVERY DAY

I believe that my life will get better and better. Any situation that is contrary to God's Word is temporary and my God will bring me victory in that area. Instead of falling for the lie that says our situation will never improve, we need to look for the promises that declare change and victory!

When we fall for the lie that says things will never get better we become despondent. Hopelessness is destructive. Hopelessness is depressing and discouraging. Hopelessness steals your joy. The Bible tells us that we can have hope because that is God's plan for us (Jeremiah 29:11). We can expect His goodness and mercy to follow us all the days of our lives (Psalms 23:6).

Isaiah 35:4 (NLT)

Say to those with fearful hearts, "Be strong, and do not fear, for your God is coming to destroy your enemies. He is coming to save you."

Take the poisonous thought that says your life will never get better and smother it with the antidote. Our fearful hearts need the truth of the Word. The truth that God is here to help us and our enemy has no authority over our amazing God.

You may be experiencing a trial right now, but remember that your God has promised victory. Your trial has an expiration date. Your trial is not permanent. During a trial, you need to speak Life into your dead situation. Jesus spoke life to Lazarus even though he had been in the tomb for four days. Jesus did not let the circumstance distract Him from the truth - and we can do the same! The same power that raised Christ from the dead is alive in us. We can operate in that power if we so choose. It is a choice. We can choose to focus on the problem and live in defeat and hopelessness, or we can choose to focus on the promises of God and live expectant and hopeful. We can choose to speak the Word of God even though our situation appears to contradict the Word. This false appearance cannot be seen in the Spirit. You must remember that there are more for you than against you despite what is visible (2 Kings 6:15-17).

More of Him, less of your circumstances. Keep your mind focused on the good things God has promised.

I AM FREE IN CHRIST

I am free! What does it mean to be free? The Greek word translated as free in this passage means to liberate; to deliver; to release; to exempt from liability or blame. Looking over this definition, who wouldn't want to walk in this freedom?

Jesus told us that the key to freedom was continuing in the Word of God. To continue means to stay, to abide, to remain present. If I want to experience Christ's freedom, then I need to abide in His Word. I need to remain present. Too many times we are in the Word, but not present. What do I mean by that? Let's look at an example. Did you ever try to hold a conversation with someone who was distracted by their cellular

John 8:31-32 (KJV)

Then said Jesus... "If ye continue in My Word, then are ye My disciples indeed; and ye shall know the truth, and the truth shall make you free."

device? They were physically there in front of you, but not present. Their body was in your vicinity, but their mind was not. We can be like that with the Word of God. We can read out of duty and really not even take in what we are reading. The Word is described as our life (Deuteronomy 32:47); we need to see it that way and treat it as such. When we understand that the Word of God is the only Seed for Spiritual fruit, we will begin to treat it with respect. The Word is not just idle words; the Word is life-giving, Spirit-filled Seeds.

As we deposit these Seeds into our hearts (minds) we will begin to experience true freedom. We will be progressively liberated from the stronghold of sin; we will progressively experience deliverance from wrong mindsets; we will begin to enjoy freedom from doubt; we will rejoice in knowing that we are guilt-free and blameless in Christ; and the list goes on thankfully. The Word of God sets us free from everything that keeps us in bondage.

If we want to experience the freedom of Christ, then we must continue in His Word. More of Him, less of me. Bondage is the result of focusing on self rather than Christ. We feel trapped by our sin, our failures, our fears, our inadequacies, and so much more, when we focus on ourselves. When He is our focus, we realize true freedom.

MY PAST IS BEHIND ME

I am free from my past because of Jesus. I don't have to dwell on it. Do you have memories that you wish you could forget? We all do. No one has led a perfect life; we all have regrets, but there is good news! We don't have to focus on those things. We can choose to replace our painful memories and regrets with the promises of God.

Life is messy. Life is real. Our God knows that; He understands that. He knew that we would struggle with sin and regret it. He prepared in advance for our struggle. He told us that we don't have to dwell on the past; instead, we could look ahead at what He is doing. He is doing a new thing! He has a fresh start waiting for you. Do you not perceive it? Do you not see His

Isaiah 43:18 (NIV)

Forget the former things; do not dwell on the past. See I am doing a new thing! Now it springs up; do you not perceive it? I am making a way in the wilderness and streams in the wasteland.

promise for forgiveness and a fresh start? This promise is a daily promise (Lamentations 3:23). He has enough compassion for each and every day of my life. That is a promise that should fill us with relief! Our sin does not have the power to keep us from our compassionate, merciful, forgiving God. Where sin abounds, His grace super-abounds! His grace is greater than my sin!

I can choose to focus on His grace or my sin. His fresh start or my past. The choice is up to me, but the choice has consequences. Focusing on His grace will fill us with thankfulness, love, joy, and peace. Focusing on our sin will fill us with fear, doubt, condemnation, and anxiety. What attributes do you want to abound in your life? The choice is ours. We've been set free from our past. It's a done deal. Christ did everything that needed to be done in order to set us free; the ball is now in our court. We have to receive His gift of freedom from the past. We have to focus on His freeing fresh start rather than our past.

More of Him, less of me. More of His forgiveness and less of my sin. More of His fresh start and less of my past. More of His promises for a life of freedom! A mind that is stayed on Him will take strangling thoughts of the past and will replace them with His life-giving promises!

I AM STRONG IN CHRIST

> **Ephesians 3:16 (KJV)**
>
> *That He would grant you, according to the riches of His glory, to be strengthened with might by His spirit in the inner man.*

I am strong *in Christ*. When I feel weak I can rest knowing that *He* is my strength. I do not have to rely on my own strength.

In Christ I have everything I need. My flesh likes to tell me lies, however. "You can't handle this." "You can't take one more thing!" "This is too hard for you!" "You are weak!" "You are weary and defeated!" These lies want to occupy our minds. These lies want to stop us from progress and from seeing victory. The Bible tells us that Satan is a liar. He is the father of lies. We need to know the truth. In and of ourselves, we *are* weak, but praise God we are not on our own!

He is our strength. We are strong in Him.

We can be strengthened in our inner man. We can receive His Word and fill ourselves with it and we can experience the strength that only He can provide.

The Bible tells us that the strong spirit of a man sustains him (Proverbs 18:14). Our spiritual strength comes from our intake of the Word. The more of the Word we ingest, the stronger we will be Spiritually and that Spiritual strength enables us to bear the trials of life like a victorious child of God. We can press on and enjoy life in spite of our circumstances when our focus is on Christ.

When Christ is my focus, I will operate in His strength. When I am focused on myself, my weaknesses will be amplified. Keep your focus on Christ. More of His strength and less of your weaknesses. More of who you are in Him and less of who you are apart from Him. When you feel weak, receive His strength! His strength will never give out.

IN CHRIST I HAVE VICTORY OVER SIN

Romans 8:9 (NLT)

But you are not controlled by your sinful nature. You are controlled by the Spirit if you have the Spirit of God living in you.

I am not a slave to sin. I do not have to let my flesh control me. Jesus Christ gave me His Spirit and His indwelling Spirit is all I need to avoid the pitfalls of sin.

Transformation will not come without truth. My flesh wants me to believe lies. This area is no different. The flesh wants us to believe that we cannot live free from the power of sin. "I just can't help it." "This is just the way I am." "I will always struggle with this." Lies like these bombard our minds but we do not have to let them reside. We can fight back and send the lies packing. We can see victory through the Word of God.

John 8:11 is the

culmination of a story about a woman caught in adultery being brought to Jesus. The legalistic leaders of the day wanted to know what Jesus thought should be done with her. Certainly she should be stoned! That was what the law said. The law highlights our sin for sure; in fact, the law was given so that sin might increase (Romans 5:20). This verse shows us that the law cannot help us avoid sin; it makes us sin more. Praise God, however, for the very next part of that verse: "...where sin abounded, grace did much more abound." Grace is translated from a Greek word that is defined as *the Divine influence upon the heart and its reflection in the life*. In other words, grace is synonymous with the Word. The Word is the Divine influence on our heart and it is reflected in our daily lives. The Word is our weapon against sin. Jesus told the woman who was caught in adultery that He did not condemn her and she could go and sin no more. He was telling her that she could find freedom from sin through Him. He was not challenging her to "behave herself" and stop sinning. He knows that we do not have that power apart from Him (and He is the Word). He was offering her the gift of freedom from sin. More of Him, less of me. Less focus on me and what I can do because apart from Him I can do nothing of Spiritual value.

NOTHING SEPARATES ME FROM MY GOD

Psalms 5:7 (NLT)

Because of Your unfailing love, I can enter Your house; I will worship at Your temple with deepest awe.

Nothing stands between me and my God. God's love for me is unfailing. It is not based on me, my actions, my circumstances, others, or anything else. God's love for me is based on Jesus Christ and that is why His love for me is unfailing and nothing can separate me from it.

My thoughts may wander from His unfailing love and cause me to doubt my relationship with God, but I need to recognize when this happens and I need to do something about it. I need to remind myself of why I am God's dearly loved child. I am God's dearly loved child because Jesus paid the price for my sin - more of Him, less of me. There is no longer a barrier between us because Christ did away with it. I have access to my Heavenly Father because of what Jesus has done for me; it is not based on me.

Our number one enemy is self. Self promotes only negative feelings: pride, arrogance, fear, and anxiety, just to name a few. As I focus on self, I will either feel self-important or self-defeated, but either way, I am self-absorbed leaving little room for God. As we trace back each of the negative mindsets we battle, we will find that we are the root of each one. For example, when I struggle with feeling like something is separating me from God, it is because I am focused on self rather than Christ. I am reminding myself of my sin instead of Christ's sacrifice and I begin to erroneously believe that God does not want to hear from me. Focusing on self will never lead us into the relationship God desires to have with us.

God's unfailing love should be our focus. His love for us provides us with access to everything we need - Him! He is everything we need. As I begin to understand this, worship is the next step. So many times we believe worship is simply singing but it is so much more. It is receiving; it is the ministration of God. He cares for us, He nurtures us, He supports for us, and so much more, as we receive through His Word - and that is awe-inspiring.

IN CHRIST I AM CONTENT

Ecclesiastes 6:9 (NIVR)

Being satisfied with what you have is better than always wanting more. That doesn't have any meaning either. It's like chasing the wind.

I can be satisfied and content with what I have. This does not mean that I am settling, but rather that I can be at ease expecting God's goodness instead of struggling and striving for more.

We all desire more, but that desire can take on a negative form leaving us discontent. Discontentment is the result of doubt. We doubt God will provide and prosper us. This doubt leaves us with a dilemma. Either we achieve all that we want ourselves or we simply settle for less than God's best. Striving to achieve leaves us exhausted and empty. We struggle to achieve believing that more will make us happy, but that is not the case. Power, position, possessions, and the like, can never make a person truly satisfied. On the other hand, settling leaves us dissatisfied, empty and frustrated.

When my mind is focused on Christ, things are not my goal. Money, possessions, status, and the like, are blessings that I can use to help my family and others, but they are not my focus. I appreciate all that I have and I realize what true wealth and success are. Having a mind that is stayed on Christ is more valuable than any possession this world can provide.

We are told in God's Word to work and work diligently. Work is not a bad thing, but it can be perverted. When we work to achieve and compete we are working in vain. We are to enjoy our labor under the sun. God has promised to give us the ability to produce wealth and provide for our families (Deuteronomy 8:18; Psalm 37:25) so we can work without stress and pressure. We can rest in God's promise to care and provide for us while we work. Our work can have purpose when Christ is our focus and it can become a blessing rather than a curse.

The world strives to achieve satisfaction but never truly does. As God's child, satisfaction is rightfully ours. We can experience true satisfaction and live life content and at peace when we focus more on Him and less on self.

IN CHRIST I UNDERSTAND THE WORD

I understand the Word of God because God has given me the ability to understand the Word.

I hear people proclaim their inability to understand the Word and I hear people declare how much they hate to read. Both of these declarations contradict the Word. Jesus came and He has given us understanding. He has given us His Spirit and we are told that we do not need a man to teach us because His Holy Spirit is our teacher (1 John 2:27). Jesus is not a liar. He is the truth and He can only speak truth. He promised us understanding so we can believe that we have the ability to understand the Word.

1 John 5:20 (NIV)

We know also that the Son of God has come and has given us understanding, so that we may know Him who is true. And we are in Him who is true by being in His Son Jesus Christ. He is the true God and eternal life.

As we voice the opposite of His promise, we begin to operate in that doubt. This disbelief leads to uncertainty. We go to the Word but we find ourselves confused. We must be aware of the fact that confusion is not from God (1 Corinthians 14:33). Confusion comes when we ignore God and what He has promised. You may struggle reading, but you can boldly declare that the struggle is temporary and has no power over you. The Word is His love letter to you; it is your mirror to show you who you are in Christ - of course He has given you the ability to understand it. Stand in that truth even when you don't feel like you are operating in it. Faith and patience will bring about the promise (Hebrews 6:12). It may take time, but it will be worth the wait.

The Son of God has come and has given us understanding so that we may know Him. As we read the Word, we become more acquainted with Christ and in becoming more aware of whom Christ is, we become more aware of whom we are. We are in Christ. As He is, so are we in this world (1 John 4:17). If we want to understand who we are, then we must learn about who He is. Our true identity is found in Him. Open His Word and read. Read knowing that you are His child and you hear His voice and you understand what He is saying.

I AM NOT INTIMIDATED

I am not intimidated because Christ is my confidence.

Intimidation is one of the enemy's favorite tactics because it is based on feelings. Feelings are fickle and they are deceptive. Feelings can be our number one enemy because feelings are unpredictable. You can feel ten different ways about a situation in less than five minutes. Feelings are like the weather and they can change without notice. When we let feelings control us we will eventually find ourselves losing control. We will experience instability and erratic behavior.

Our feelings are not always based on facts. Many times they are based on appearances and irrational

Philippians 1:28 (NLT)

Don't be intimidated in any way by your enemies. This will be a sign to them that they are going to be destroyed, but that you are going to be saved, even by God Himself.

thoughts. When we let our feelings control us, then we are open for attack. The enemy encourages feelings of terror and inadequacy as he lies to us about our circumstances. He plays the "What If?" game with us until we are terrified and panicked about something that most likely will never happen. If the enemy can get you to feel afraid and pathetic, then he sees the finish line. He smells blood in the water and he prepares to go for the jugular. We can avoid this attack, however.

Intimidation does not have to persuade us. We can control our feelings by keeping our mind stayed on Christ. We can rule over our feelings. We can choose to focus on the promises of God when our feelings begin to take over. We can choose the Word. We can ignore fear and inadequacy when we look at Christ. More of Him, less of our situation. More of Him, less of us. We may feel inadequate, but He is all-sufficient. How can I feel as if I am lacking when I am focused on Him? In Him I have everything I need for life and godliness (2 Peter 1:3). How can I feel fearful when I know my God is with me? He will calm all my fears with His love (Zephaniah 3:17 NLT).

The enemy is a defeated foe because of Christ. We will see him that way when we focus more on Christ

I AM AT REST BECAUSE OF CHRIST

I am at rest because of Christ. He is kind, good, and merciful.

The Hebrew word translated as rest is defined as a settled spot, a home, a place of rest, quiet. It is such a beautiful and peaceful description. Just reading the definition invokes a feeling of ease. Hearing the words "a settled spot" reminds me of my favorite place on the couch. A place where I can relax, put my feet up, and feel cozy. This spot on the couch is where I like to settle for the evening. I feel at ease. I am at rest. I am not worried or concerned about taking care of anything. I am simply relaxed. This is how God wants us to feel at all times. How wonderful is our God!

Psalm 116:5, 7 (NLT)

How kind the Lord is! How good He is! So merciful, this God of ours! Let my soul be at rest again, for the Lord has been good to me.

We can experience this rest when we realize how good our God is. He is kind. He is merciful. He is full of grace. He knows that we are dust and He knows how much we need Him so He has freely given of Himself. I can be at rest when I realize that He is everything I need. When I am afraid, He is my courage. When I am weak, He is my strength. When I am uncertain, He is my assurance. When I am grieving, He is my comfort. When I am sad, He is my joy. I can go on and on. He is my everything. We forget this when we focus on self. More of Him, less of me. If I want to be at rest, my mind must be stayed on Him. I cannot experience rest when I am self-centered. Rest is the result of focusing on God and His goodness.

God has been SO good to us! Sadly, we need reminded of this fact. Too many times we let life lie to us. We make our problems bigger than our blessings by focusing on them instead of God's goodness. Are you breathing today? Thank God for His goodness! Start there and go down the list. We could give thanks all day long and never even scratch the surface of His goodness.

More of Him, less of me. More of His blessings and less of my complaints. More of His goodness and less of my drama. I can be at rest when I focus on Him.

I HAVE SELF-CONTROL IN CHRIST

God has gifted me with self-control. I am not out of control when I am focused on Him.

I cannot count the number of times I have heard myself say, "I can't help myself!" That is such a lie. A lie that the enemy wants us to believe whole-heartedly. When we believe that we are out of control we begin to feel hopeless. Fear also creeps up on us when we feel a lack of control. Hopelessness and fear are both paralyzing. They keep us focused on self rather than Christ, and that is where we will always experience defeat.

My life is a gift from God and I must treat it that way. I need to realize that He longs for me to enjoy the abundant life that

*2 Timothy
1:7 (ESV)*

For God

gave us

a spirit not

of fear but

of power

and love

and

self-control.

He has gifted me with. As long as I feel like I am out of control, abundant life will elude me. We must realize that God has given us His Spirit and His Spirit does not lack control. We have self-control because He lives in us; it is a fruit of His Spirit. When we begin to feel out of control, we need to remind ourselves that self-control is ours through Jesus Christ. I *can* calm down; I *can* be nice; I *can* ignore insults; I *can* stick to my diet; I *can* do all things through Christ who gives me the strength and self-control I lack apart from Him.

When we buy into the lie that says we can't, we are ignoring the gift of self-control. God's gifts were meant to be received, not ignored. We receive every good and perfect gift from God through His Word. Focus on His promise of self-control when you don't feel it at work in your life. Meditate on His promise instead of your lack.

More of Him, less of me. More of what He has freely given, less of what I feel I lack. Jesus loves me. He loves me so much that He has given me everything I will ever need. He knew I would struggle. He knew I would feel helpless and fearful and out of control so He provided me with everything I need to demolish those feelings. His Word is my weapon and I must use it if I want to walk in the self-control He has freely provided.

I APPRECIATE TODAY

I appreciate each and every day I am alive. I realize that life is short so I make the most of today.

Life is often taken for granted. We walk through our days without appreciating what is right in front of us. We complain about so much when we should be voicing our thankfulness. We whine about our job instead of thanking God for gainful employment. We grumble about standing in line at the grocery store instead of thanking God for food to eat. We moan and groan about cleaning our homes instead of thanking God for the roof over our head and the family inside. The list can go on and on. We voice incessant complaints when really there is so much to be thankful for. Life is to be

Psalms 90:12 (NLT)

Teach us to realize the brevity of life, so that we may grow in wisdom.

embraced and appreciated. Life is God's gift. No one knows when their time here will be over. Treating each day like it could be our last is not just some memorable adage; it is a nugget of wisdom that will change your life.

Those who are wise realize that life is brief and it is to be embraced. We are wise in Christ. Jesus Christ is our wisdom. When we live life focused on Him we will appreciate life and we will value each day we have here. We will make the most of this life as we look forward to heaven. It is when we begin to focus on self that life becomes drudgery. Selfishness breeds misery. A selfish life is a wretched life. When we are self-absorbed we will never experience true joy. God's Word tells us that complete joy is found in His presence - not ours (Psalms 16:11)! If we want to live a life of joy, then our minds must be stayed on Christ. More of Him, less of me. That will always be the theme for every Spirit-filled life.

Today is a gift from God and what we do with it is up to us. How we choose to view the day will determine how much we will enjoy the day. It is time for us to realize that each day is to be embraced and appreciated. My life is special because of Christ. My life is valuable because of Christ. My life is a wonderful gift and I am going to choose to focus on Christ and make the most of it.

I AM THANKFUL; I AM JOYFUL

My life is full of joy because I am thankful. I realize what God is doing for me and I am joyful.

I don't think we'll ever fully comprehend all that God has done for us until we reach the other side of eternity. The ability to breathe is a multi-faceted blessing that we cannot even grasp completely and it's something we're constantly blessed with. Do we stop to thank God for the ability to breathe? Most of the time we take it for granted. How would life change if we lived thankful?

Thankful people are joyful people. When we realize how good God is and we live thankful lives, joy will flow. Joy is a fruit of the Spirit. It is experienced

Psalms 92:4 (NLT)

You thrill me, Lord, with all You have done for me! I sing for joy because of what You have done.

when we focus on Christ. As we focus on Christ, we will see all the good things He has blessed us with.

Joy is not something we decide to have. Again, it is a fruit of the Spirit, and like every other fruit, it is only produced by the Seed of the Word. As we plant the Seed of the Word in our hearts, joy will begin to grow in our lives. Joy is the result of the Word. Joy is based on Jesus Christ. I can live a joyful life when I am focused on Christ rather than self.

Focusing on self leaves us lacking. We are not complete without Christ. We will lack joy without Him - not to mention satisfaction, worth, peace, strength, love, faith, and every other Spiritual fruit that there is.

Are you *thrilled* with all that the Lord has done for you? Do you take the time to count your blessings and remind yourself of all that God has done? Trials tend to keep us from giving thanks and from experiencing the joy of the Lord. They do this because they tend to capture our attention. When trials come we are tempted to think about our situation rather than God's promises. As we lose focus on the Word, joy slips away slowly but surely. Joy is found in His presence; we need to remain focused on the Word if we want to experience His joy. More of Him, less of me. More of what I have to be thankful for.

I AM HUMBLE

I am humble. I realize that I have nothing to boast about outside of Jesus Christ.

As Christians, we are so blessed and there are times when we take those blessings for granted and there are times when we try to take credit for those blessings. We erroneously believe that we somehow deserve God's goodness when it is a free gift thanks to Jesus Christ and Him alone. The Message Bible tells us not to "put on airs," or, in other words, don't be prideful. We cannot take credit for the Spiritual fruit in our lives. It is only realized because of Christ. We plant the Seed of His Word and *He* makes it grow. We cannot understand the process, but He does (Mark 4:27). He is

> *1 Peter 5:6-7 (MSG)*
>
> *So be content with who you are, and don't put on airs. God's strong hand is on you; He'll promote you at the right time. Live carefree before God; He is most careful with you.*

the reason we experience the fruit of the Spirit in our lives. He is the Source of every good thing we have.

We can be humble and content with who we are when we realize *God's* strong hand is at work in our lives. Our God is strong; His strength overcomes our weakness when we look to Him. He has a plan for us and it is good (Jeremiah 29:11)! His good plan will be realized at the right time - His perfect time. We can live carefree instead of living in worry and doubt when we understand that God is working all things together for our good (Romans 8:28) because He loves us, not because we deserve it.

"He is most careful with you." What a beautiful statement. This statement should flood us with the love of God. He cares so much. His love for us is never-ending and unfailing. When you feel like you are full of care, take the time to remind yourself of His love for you. Look up verses that talk about His love and meditate on them. His love will swallow up your fear and doubt. He is most careful with you so you can be carefree. Cast all your cares on Him; He is willing to shoulder them because He cares for you (1 Peter 5:7). He knows we cannot carry that burden so, in His love, He carries it for us. That should humble us. We *cannot* carry this load; we need Him. More of Him, less of me. That is a life of humility.

I AM EXPECTING GOD'S BEST TODAY

The best is yet to come. I am expecting God's good promises to flood my life!

We are on our way to all the good things God has promised. One day we will see the culmination of God's Word when we join our beloved Savior in our heavenly home; but until then, we can begin to experience heaven here on earth.

The Lord has promised wonderful blessings. These blessings are meant to be enjoyed now throughout eternity. Are you on your way? Are you looking to the Word and meditating on God's good promises or are you focused on your current situation? Your current situation is temporary if

Numbers 10:29 (NLT)

...we are on our way to the place the Lord promised us, for He said, "I will give it to you!" ...the Lord has promised wonderful blessings...

it does not agree with God's Word. You may have to go through some things that disagree with the Word, but those things are a means to an end. The Red Sea seemed like a barrier; it looked to be a hindrance but it was in fact a pathway to better things (Psalms 77:19). You may not be able to see your trial as a pathway, but it is. You are not meant to live below God's best. Anything that disagrees with His Word is transitory; you are passing through. We may have to walk through the flood waters, but He promises that we will not drown (Isaiah 43:2). This world may be full of trials, but we can look ahead and focus on the promises of God. We can be joyful and full of cheer when we focus on the fact that our God has overcome the world and deprived it of power over us (John 16:33).

More of Him, less of me. That is the theme of a transformed life. A mind that is stayed on Christ will keep us peaceful and expectant. Are you expecting good things or more of the same old negatives? You can focus on the good promises of God if you want to. It is up to you. What areas are you living below God's best? Take each area and look up at least 3 verses that promise you something better. Focus on those promises and watch your expectancy change. Good things are ahead! Enjoy the good things by focusing more on Him, less on self.

The Two of Me

Have you ever felt like two people in one body? Have you ever wondered why you do what you do? Do you ever feel like you are at war with yourself?

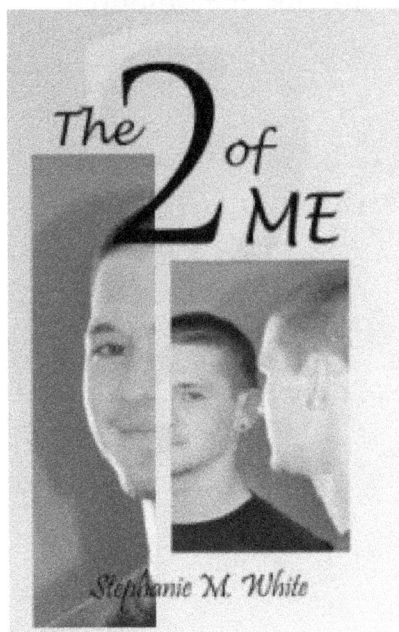

As Christians, we must understand that we have two natures - our Spiritual nature and our flesh. Each nature wants to dominate, but only one can. This book will take you through a thorough study of your two natures and it will help you understand each one. It will also show you how to rule over your flesh and defeat its power in your life.

https://www.amazon.com/gp/product/0982874332/ref=dbs_a_def_rwt_bibl_vppi_i0

https://whitestephanie83.wixsite.com/heavenonearthforyou

We hope that you enjoyed 31 Days of Just Jesus.

Please visit our website for more Christian resources that focus solely on Jesus Christ.

https://whitestephanie83.wixsite.com/ heavenonearthforyou

Off-Season

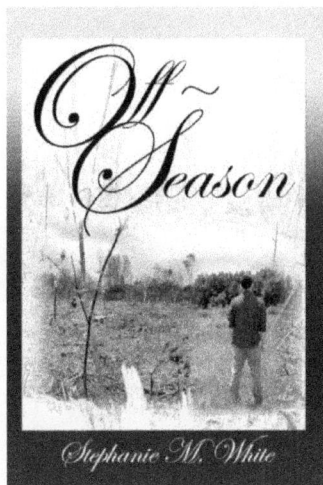

Everyone experiences an off-season in life - sometimes more than one. An off-season is a dry time; it is a time of lack and a time of trials. These times can feel daunting and painful; therefore, we must understand the purpose of these times and we must be sure that God has a plan for our good and His glory.

https://whitestephanie83.wixsite.com/heavenonearthforyou

https://www.amazon.com/Stephanie-White/e/B001K86MBC

https://www.amazon.com/gp/product/0989697304/ref=dbs_a_def_rwt_bibl_vppi_i1

MORE BOOKS by STPHANIE M. WHITE

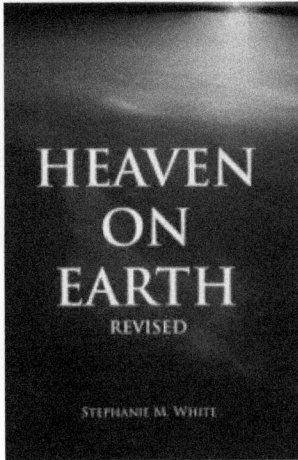

Heaven on Earth: it is a life most people believe is not possible to achieve, but according to God's Word that is exactly what we can have! Heaven on Earth takes you on a journey through the Word of God so that you can find out what is available to you as God's child and you will also discover how to enjoy this life to the fullest.

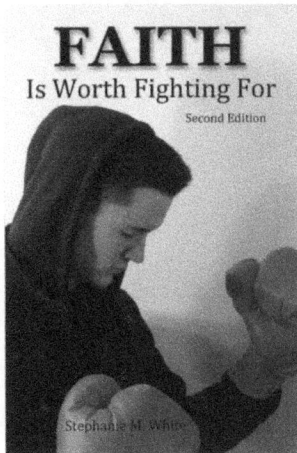

In God's Word we discover that we are to live by faith, but we also see that faith is a fight. As a Christian, faith is essential. Eternal value is assigned to our faith. This book is an in-depth study of faith - what faith is, how we obtain it, how it works, what classifies it as genuine, what its benefits are, and more.

https://www.amazon.com/Stephanie-White/e/B001K86MBC

A SEASON OF GRIEF
is a unique devotional designed to facilitate those who have suffered loss and are grieving.

Grief can bring even the strongest to their knees. As we endure a season of grief we will experience a myriad of emotions that we cannot ignore. As you read through this devotional you will find encouragement to deal with these feelings and move forward in spite of them because you are abiding in the Word of God.

We must invite Christ into our season of grief; we must take in His Word and receive the healing that only He can provide.

Our loved ones who have gone on ahead of us want us to enjoy the life that we have left; they want us to remember them and smile and look forward to being reunited with them.

The Word of God is our life. It is meant to be our daily life. This devotional will help you incorporate the Word of God into your life even as you press past the pain of loss.

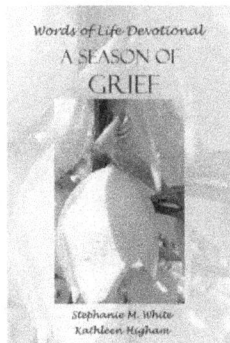

Words of Life Devotional
A SEASON OF GRIEF

Stephanie M. White
Kathleen Higham

A NEW BEGINNING

A New Beginning

New Christian Devotional

Stephanie M. White

If you enjoyed this **31 Days of Just Jesus** devotional, please order your copy of our **A New Beginning** devotional.

Whether you are a new Christian, or have been saved for years, this devotional will remind you of fundamental truths that we all need to be sure of.

https://whitestephanie83.wixsite.com/heavenonearthforyou

https://www.amazon.com/Stephanie-White/e/B001K86MBC

www.ingramcontent.com/pod-product-compliance
Lightning Source LLC
Chambersburg PA
CBHW020955030426
42339CB00005B/112